Planet Earth

Planet Earth

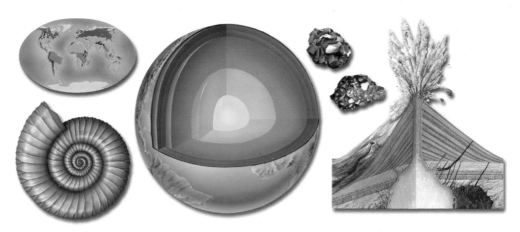

Brian Williams

Miles Kelly

PUBLISHING

Author
Brian Williams

Designed, Edited and Project Managed by
Starry Dog Books

Editor
Belinda Gallagher

Assistant Editor
Mark Darling

Artwork Commissioning
Lesley Cartlidge

Indexer
Janet De Saulles

Art Director
Clare Sleven

Editorial Director
Paula Borton

First published in 2001 by
Miles Kelly Publishing Ltd
The Bardfield Centre
Great Bardfield
Essex CM7 4SL

2468109753

Some material in this book can also be found in *The Greatest Book of the Biggest and Best*

A British Library Cataloguing-in-Publication Data.
A catalogue record for this book is available from the British Library

ISBN 1-84236-029-9
Printed in China

www.mileskelly.net
info@mileskelly.net

CONTENTS

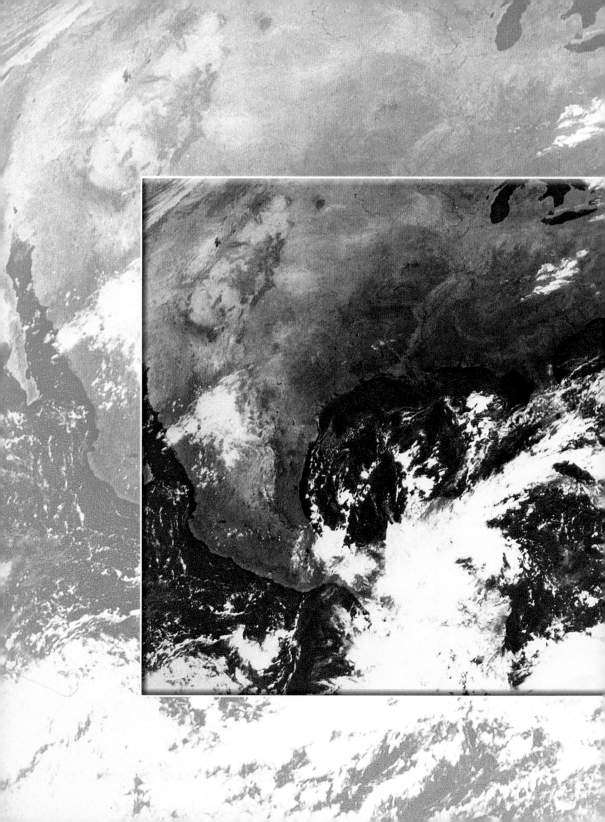

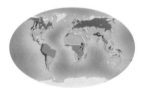

PLANET EARTH

*O*ur planet really is an amazing place. More than two thirds of it is covered by oceans, yet there are vast areas of burning desert, mountains of unimaginable height, hot, steamy rainforests and an exotic array of animal life.

It is these fantastic features of the Earth that provide us with some amazing statistics. For instance, our planet is solid ball of rock, 6,400 km thick. Yet the inner core is so hot, the rock within it is molten, reaching an incredible temperature of more than 4,000ºC. All around us are amazing things we take for granted; water recycling and falling as rain, the movement of the Earth's plates beneath our feet, grumbling volcanoes and beautiful rainbows. Within this book stunning images of these amazing natural features are accompanied by facts you'll never forget.

Explore the biggest and best facts about *Planet Earth* and rediscover your planet. There are the big, serious facts – for reference – and less serious ones, too, for fun. These pages are packed with the biggest and best, oddest and strangest, smallest and funniest facts around!

EARTH FACTS

Earth is a ball of rock mostly covered by water and wrapped in a thin, protective layer of gases – the air. It was formed at the same time as the Sun and the other planets, about 4.6 billion years ago. The outer layer of Earth is called the crust. All the continents and seas lie on the crust. Underneath the crust is the mantle, made of molten rock that moves very slowly. As it moves, huge pieces of the crust, called continental plates, move too.

crust,
5 to 50 km thick

▲ Zircon crystals found in Australia are 4,276 million years old – the oldest part of Earth's crust ever discovered.

landmass

◄ Some 280 million years ago all the continents were joined in one huge landmass, called Pangaea. Over time, this 'super-continent' broke up and the landmasses drifted apart to form the continents we know today.

▼ Earth's rocky skin, the crust, is thickest – about 50 km thick – beneath 'young' or recently built mountain ranges such as the Himalayas in Asia. The crust beneath the oceans is much thinner, between 5 to 11 km thick.

ocean

continental plate movement

»» ■ EARTH'S LAYERS		
Atmosphere	Gases	80 to 1,600 km thick
Earth's crust	Rocks	5 to 50 km thick
Mantle	Rocks	About 2,800 km thick
Core	Melted rocks	About 3,550 km thick

quartz

galena

pyrite

gypsum

barite

calcite

upper mantle

lower mantle

outer core

inner core

distance to the centre of Earth is 6,400 km

deepest hole yet drilled was 1,200 km deep

▲ *Earth is made of rocks. Rocks are themselves made of a mass of minerals like the ones shown here. Usually minerals are formed as crystals. Some, such as gypsum, are soft. Others, like quartz, are very hard and can scratch glass.*

LARGEST LANDMASSES

	CONTINENT	AREA
1	Asia	44,009,000 sq km
2	Africa	30,246,000 sq km
3	North America	24,219,000 sq km
4	South America	17,832,000 sq km
5	Europe	10,443,000* sq km
6	Australia	7,713,000 sq km

* Europe is joined to Asia, so the two are sometimes called Eurasia

◄ *Although Earth looks round, it has a bulge just south of the Equator. It spins on its axis – an imaginary line between the Poles. The centre of Earth is about 6,400 km from the surface. The deeper down inside Earth, the hotter it gets. At Earth's core it is so hot – over 4,000°C – that the rocks there are molten rather than solid.*

EARTH FACTS

Equatorial circumference	40,075 km
Polar circumference	40,008 km
Surface area	509,700,000 sq km
Land area	29 percent
Water area	71 percent
Most abundant chemical	oxygen (47% of mass)

AWESOME OCEANS

Viewed from space, Earth looks like a watery world. More than 70 percent of the planet is covered by water, and about 97 percent of all Earth's water is in the oceans. These cover more than 360 million sq km. The Pacific is the biggest ocean. It is twice as big as the next largest ocean, the Atlantic. It also has the biggest waves and the deepest deeps, but not the highest tides. These are in the Bay of Fundy on the Atlantic coast of North America.

»	THE BIGGEST OCEANS	
	OCEAN	AREA
★ 1	Pacific	181 million sq km
2	Atlantic	94 million sq km
3	Indian	74 million sq km

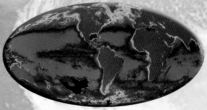

▲ The world's oceans are not all the same temperature. This map shows the warm and cold waters in the top 100 m of the oceans. Deeper down, warm and cold currents swirl a few metres a day in great circular patterns, driven by the saltiness of the water.

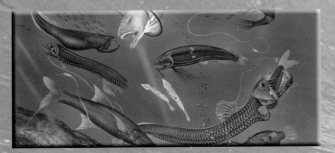

▲ Sunlight never reaches below 200 m, but thousands of metres down in the darkest depths, some fish have bodies that glow. Some even have luminous tentacles used to lure prey.

▶ In 1961 the US navy sent a manned deep-sea diving machine, a bathyscaphe called Trieste, to the bottom of the Marianas Trench in the Pacific. At 10,911 m deep, this is the deepest point in any of the world's oceans.

bathyscaphes are used to explore the ocean bed 6,000 m below the surface of the sea

deep sea trench

»	LONGEST OCEAN TRENCHES		
	TRENCH	OCEAN	LENGTH
★ 1	Peru-Atacama	Pacific	3,540 km
2	Aleutian	Pacific	3,200 km
3	Tonga-Kermadec	Pacific	2,575 km
4	Marianas	Pacific	2,250 km
5	Philippine	Pacific	1,325 km

DEEPEST OCEAN TRENCHES

	TRENCH	OCEAN	DEPTH
1	Marianas	Pacific	10,911 m
2	Tonga-Kermadec	Pacific	10,882 m
3	Philippine	Pacific	10,497 m
4	Bonin	Pacific	9,994 m
5	New Britain	Pacific	9,940 m

▲ *Waves are blown along by winds. The highest wave ever seen was in 1933, when a US navy ship was caught in a Pacific hurricane and survived a wave estimated to be 34 m high. Waves three times higher can be caused by undersea earthquakes.*

EXTREME WATERS

Deepest	Pacific Ocean
Shallowest	Atlantic Ocean
Coldest	Arctic Ocean
Warmest	Persian Gulf

◀ *Canada has the longest coastline of any country. Including the many islands, the coast is more than 244,000 km long – that is six times longer than the coast of Australia.*

▼ *Underneath the oceans is a dramatic landscape that is rarely seen. Mountains rise up, sometimes breaking the surface of the water as islands. There are also deep trenches. The Marianas Trench in the Pacific is the deepest, dwarfing the famous Grand Canyon in the USA.*

continental shelf

muddy sediment left by river currents

continental slope

ocean ridge

RECORD RIVERS

Did you know that all the water on Earth is constantly recycled? The first downpour lasted for thousands of years, more than three billion years ago. It filled the oceans and seas. The warmth of the Sun makes water in the oceans 'evaporate' or turn into water vapour in the air. The water vapour is blown over land by the wind. As the moist air rises over hills, it cools and turns into water droplets that fall as rain or snow. The rainwater finds its way into streams and rivers, which return it to the oceans.

»	LONGEST RIVERS	
	RIVER	LOCATION
1	Nile	Africa
2	Amazon	S. America
3	Chang Jiang (Yangtze)	China
4	Huang He (Yellow)	China
5	Congo (Zaire)	Africa

▲ *The Amazon River in South America, shown here, carries more water than any other river, although it is slightly shorter than the Nile River in northern Africa.*

◀ *The Colorado River flows for 2,200 km across the United States and into Mexico. Over millions of years it has gouged out the spectacular 1.6-km-deep Grand Canyon.*

water from oceans and lakes evaporates

DID YOU KNOW?

The Suez canal was opened in 1869. This 'river through the sand' was the biggest engineering feat of its time, linking the Mediterranean and Red Seas. Ships steaming from Europe to India no longer had to go around Africa – a saving of 7,000 km.

▲ *White water rafting through rapids is thrilling and dangerous. Rapids occur where rivers flow fast over soft rock, from which boulders of harder rock stick up, making the water swirl.*

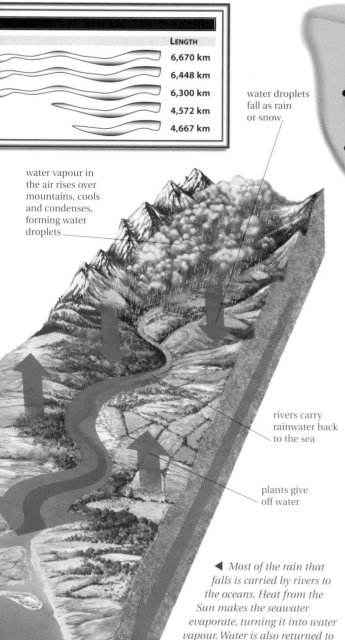

	LENGTH
	6,670 km
	6,448 km
	6,300 km
	4,572 km
	4,667 km

water droplets
fall as rain
or snow

water vapour in
the air rises over
mountains, cools
and condenses,
forming water
droplets

rivers carry
rainwater back
to the sea

plants give
off water

RECORD RIVERS

- The longest river in Europe is the Volga, at 3,531 km.
- The longest river in the United States is the Missouri, at 4,090 km.
- The longest river in Australia is the Darling, at 2,739 km.
- The muddiest river is the Huang He, or Yellow River, in China.

◀ *People have travelled up and down rivers, transporting goods, ever since the ancient Egyptians first sailed craft like this boat, called a felucca, along the Nile River more than 5,000 years ago.*

IT'S A FACT
The first great civilizations all grew up beside rivers, because crops could be grown in the fertile soils. Egypt's civilization developed along the Nile River (its delta is shown here). Mesopotamia's civilization started between the Tigris and Euphrates Rivers, and the Indus civilization grew along the Indus River.

◀ *Most of the rain that falls is carried by rivers to the oceans. Heat from the Sun makes the seawater evaporate, turning it into water vapour. Water is also returned to the atmosphere by plants. When water vapour cools it forms clouds, which release the water as rain, and the cycle begins again.*

WATERFALLS

Waterfalls happen when a river flows over a band of hard rock that is lying on top of softer rock. Because the softer rock wears away more quickly than the hard rock, the hard rock sticks out like a ledge with nothing underneath it. As the river flows over the ledge, the water falls with a thunderous roar and clouds of drenching spray in a thrilling spectacle.

» HIGHEST FALLS

	Falls	Country	Drop
★ 1	Angel	Venezuela	979 m
2	Tugela	Africa	947 m
3	Utigård	Norway	800 m
4	Mongefossen	Norway	774 m
5	Yosemite	USA	739 m
6	Østre Mardøla Foss	Norway	656 m

▲ The highest falls are the Angel Falls in Venezuela, South America. One 'drop' is 807 m, and the total drop is 979 m – more than twice the height of the Empire State Building.

▲ The Victoria Falls on the Zambezi River in Zimbabwe, Africa, are 108 m high. They were named 'the smoke that thunders' by the local people.

▲ The Iguaçu Falls between Argentina and Brazil are spectacularly wide at 3 km. They have a total drop of 80 m.

DID YOU KNOW?
When salmon are fully grown, they return from the sea to breed in the same rivers in which they were born. After finding their way back to the river's mouth, they swim upstream, defying rapids and small waterfalls. They leap and twist to find a way through the cascading torrents of water. If a dam blocks their way, the fish swim through its tunnels to reach the higher stretch of river.

➤➤	FALLS WITH THE MOST WATER			
	FALLS	RIVER	COUNTRY	FLOW
1	Boyoma	Congo	Congo	17,000 cu m per sec
2	Guaira	Paraná	Brazil/Paraguay	13,000 cu m per sec
3	Khone	Mekong	Laos	12,000 cu m per sec
4	Niagara	Niagara	Canada/USA	6,000 cu m per sec

▼ The world-famous Niagara Falls are on the border between the USA and Canada. There are two sections, the American Falls, at 320 m wide, and the Canadian or Horseshoe Falls, at 675 m wide. The falls are gradually retreating upstream. Over the last 10,000 years they have worn away 11 km of rock. The Terrapin Tower, shown here, was built next to the Horseshoe Falls in 1829, but was blown up in 1872!

LAKES AND INLAND SEAS

A lake is a big expanse of water surrounded by land. Some lakes are so big they are called inland seas. Most lake water is fresh rather than salty, but in some lakes so much water is lost by evaporation – it turns into water vapour as it is heated by the Sun – that the remaining water tastes very salty. The saltiest inland sea is the Dead Sea. Evaporation can cause some inland seas to shrink in hot weather. Australia's biggest lake, Lake Eyre, is dry for years and fills with water only after unusually heavy rains.

▲ *The 725-km-long St Lawrence Seaway, a great commercial waterway, links the Great Lakes of North America and the Atlantic Ocean.*

▼ *Loch Ness – loch means lake – in Scotland, is best known for its 'monster'. There have been many reported sightings and hoax pictures of the strange creature, but no firm evidence of its existence.*

➤➤ LARGEST LAKES/INLAND SEAS	
LAKE/SEA	**AREA**
★ 1 Caspian Sea	371,000 sq km
2 Lake Superior	82,350 sq km
3 Lake Victoria	69,500 sq km
4 Aral Sea	66,500 sq km
5 Lake Huron	59,600 sq km

NORTH AMERICA

Lake Huron

Lake Superior

SOUTH AMERICA

▶ *High in the Andes Mountains of Peru, straddling the border with Bolivia, is Lake Titicaca – the highest navigable lake in the world. It is 3,810 m above sea level.*

▲ *Lake Titicaca is a vast expanse of blue water surrounded by snow-capped peaks. It is home to the native Indians, who live in floating villages made from huge reed rafts. They also make crescent-shaped boats from the reeds that grow thickly in the marshy shallows.*

▶ *Lake Baikal in Siberia, Russia, is about 25 million years old. It is 1,637 m deep and contains about one-fifth of all the world's fresh water. The water is carried there by 336 rivers that flow into it. Lake Baikal has the world's only freshwater seals, and among its many unique animals is a fish that bears live young.*

▼ *The Dead Sea in Israel and Jordan is well named. This saltwater lake is the lowest lake on Earth – about 400 m below sea level. In summer scorching heat causes high evaporation, making the water so salty that a person cannot sink, and any fish entering the lake from the Jordan River die instantly. Only bacteria can survive.*

EUROPE

ASIA

AFRICA

Caspian Sea

Aral Sea

Lake Baikal

Lake Victoria

Lake Tanganyika

Lake Nyasa

AUSTRALASIA

LONGEST LAKES/INLAND SEAS		
	Lake/Sea	Length
★ 1	Caspian Sea	1,201 km
2	Lake Tanganyika	676 km
3	Lake Baikal	636 km
4	Lake Nyasa	580 km
5	Lake Superior	563 km

▼ *The Caspian Sea is the biggest lake in the world. But it is getting smaller because more water is being taken out for irrigation than flows into it from rivers.*

THE GREAT LAKES OF NORTH AMERICA		
	Lake	Rank
★ 1	Superior	World's biggest freshwater lake
2	Huron	5th largest freshwater lake
3	Michigan	6th largest freshwater lake
4	Erie	6th largest in North America
5	Ontario	8th largest in North America

ISLANDS AND REEFS

Islands are made in different ways. Some are the tops of undersea mountains or volcanoes. Others, such as the British Isles, were once part of a large landmass, but became surrounded by sea when the water level rose. A chain of islands is called an archipelago. The world's biggest archipelago is Indonesia, with more than 13,000 islands. Reefs are made from the bodies of millions of tiny coral animals. In warm seas they often form rings around small islands.

▲ *The biggest island in the world is Greenland, at 2,670 km long and 1,210 km wide. It is owned by Denmark, but is 50 times bigger. Greenland is 85 percent covered by ice and has very little greenery!*

ISLAND OR CONTINENT?

● Australia is bigger than Greenland, but is usually classed as a continent, not an island.

● The 13,000 islands of Indonesia stretch over a distance of 5,600 km.

▶ *New islands can appear out of the sea. Surtsey Island off Iceland rose from the waves following a volcanic eruption as recently as 1963. It grew to a height of 170 m in three years.*

▼ *When volcanoes erupt under the sea, new islands may appear. 1) Molten rock breaks through Earth's crust. 2) As more lava is deposited on the sea bed, a cone shape builds up. 3) When this breaks the water's surface, a new island appears. The volcano may go on erupting.*

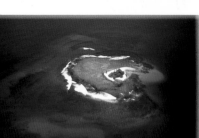

◀ *There are thousands of tiny islands in the Pacific Ocean. Many are ringed by coral reefs. Sometimes a volcanic island sinks, and all that is left is a ring of coral, called an atoll.*

1   2

» TOP FIVE ISLANDS

	ISLAND	OCEAN	AREA
★1	Greenland	Atlantic/Arctic	2.2 million sq km
2	New Guinea	Pacific	821,000 sq km
3	Borneo	Indian	744,000 sq km
4	Madagascar	Indian	587,000 sq km
5	Baffin	Arctic	476,000 sq km

▶ *The biggest coral reef on Earth is the Great Barrier Reef off eastern Australia. It is 2,000 km long, and is made from over 400 different corals. The reef has taken more than 2 million years to form.*

▲ *The tiny 20-km-long Manhattan Island in the heart of New York City, USA, is now a forest of skyscrapers, where once there were only trees. A Dutch settler bought the island in 1626 from some Native Americans for a few dollars-worth of trinkets.*

▲ *A coral reef is a rich habitat for wildlife. It provides food and shelter for dazzling tropical fish.*

▲ *Coral is the skeletons of tiny sea animals called polyps. Some polyps can grow to be 30 cm across.*

MASSIVE MOUNTAINS

Mountains are made by movements within Earth's rocky crust. The crust is made up of rigid plates that move as the mantle beneath the crust slowly moves. The highest mountains are the youngest and are still growing. They are pushed up by enormous pressure from deep inside Earth. The highest mountain on land is Mount Everest in the Himalayas of Asia. An even higher peak, Mauna Kea in Hawaii, rises out of the sea and is a volcanic mountain. The longest range or chain of mountains is the Andes in South America.

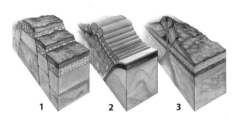

▲ 1) A fault mountain is made when weak points in Earth's crust crack and whole areas sink or are forced upwards.
2) A fold mountain is made when parts of Earth's crust shift and layers of rock are forced up into folds.
3) A volcano mountain is made as the lava that flows out cools and hardens.

	THE BIG FIVE PEAKS	
	MOUNTAIN	**HEIGHT**
1	Everest (shown here)	8,848 m
2	K2	8,610 m
3	Kanchenjunga	8,598 m
4	Lhotse	8,511 m
5	Makalu	8,481 m

Note: All these mountains are in the Himalayas

▶ The Eiger in Switzerland is 3,970 m high, and it challenges the very best climbers. First climbed in 1858, its towering north face was not scaled until 1938.

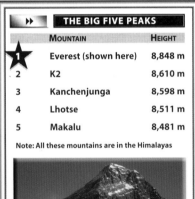

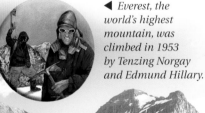

◀ Everest, the world's highest mountain, was climbed in 1953 by Tenzing Norgay and Edmund Hillary.

▼ The Rocky Mountain ranges run north–south across most of western North America. These sharp peaks in Montana have been shaped by sheets of ice called glaciers.

HIGHEST MOUNTAINS BY CONTINENT

	Mountain	Location	Height
1	Everest	Asia	8,848 m
2	Aconcagua	South America	6,960 m
3	McKinley	North America	6,194 m
4	Kilimanjaro	Africa	5,895 m
5	Elbrus	Europe	5,633 m
6	Vinson	Antarctica	5,140 m
7	Cook	Oceania	3,764 m

▶ *The Andes is the longest mountain range, stretching for 7,200 km along the western side of South America. The highest peak is Aconcagua in Argentina. It is 6,960 m high.*

MOUNTAIN MARVELS

● The Himalayas have the world's 20 highest mountains. They are all over 8,000 m high.

● The Andes range has 50 peaks over 6,000 m high, making it the biggest in the Americas.

● Snowcapped Mount Kilimanjaro (shown here) in Tanzania is the highest mountain in Africa.

● The highest mountains in North America are in Alaska, USA, and the Yukon, Canada.

▼ *Mountain goats live on the steep cliffs and glacier edges of the Rocky Mountains. They prefer areas of high snowfall.*

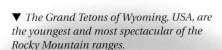

▼ *The Grand Tetons of Wyoming, USA, are the youngest and most spectacular of the Rocky Mountain ranges.*

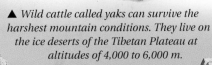

▲ *Wild cattle called yaks can survive the harshest mountain conditions. They live on the ice deserts of the Tibetan Plateau at altitudes of 4,000 to 6,000 m.*

▲ *The chamois is a European goat-antelope. Incredibly agile, it can run along the narrowest ledges and near-vertical slopes.*

CAVERNOUS CAVES

Caves are holes in the ground, usually hollowed out by water. Rainwater trickles down through the ground and dissolves the minerals in rocks such as limestone, forming hollows and tunnels. Some caves are very long passages, and some are huge open spaces called caverns. But much more common are 'pot-holes', which are deep, narrow passages, sometimes leading to caverns. Explorers crawl through pot-holes on hands and knees, or even swim through flooded sections of a cave, using flashlights to penetrate the gloom.

▲ Prehistoric people lived in caves, and some caves contain pictures of animals made by these cave-dwellers. Stone Age people drew cave paintings of hunting scenes at Lascaux in France more than 15,000 years ago.

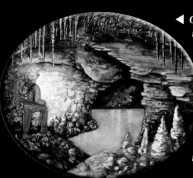

◀ Cave explorers, or cavers, wear helmets and tough clothing, as caves are often wet and cold, and rocks can be sharp. For safety they explore in groups. Each caver carries at least two torches, one fixed to the helmet so the caver's hands are free.

▲ The world's longest caves are the Mammoth Caves of Kentucky, USA, first explored in 1799. This cave system has 560 km of caves and passages, with underground lakes and rivers. The second-longest cave system, in Ukraine, extends for 156 km.

◀ In the limestone Carlsbad Caverns of New Mexico, USA, the most weird and wonderful stalactites and stalagmites can be seen. The Big Room is a huge underground chamber measuring 550 m long and 335 m wide.

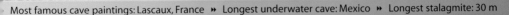

▶ *Cave animals include bats, birds and even fish. Bats roost in caves, often in huge numbers, sleeping upside down by day and leaving the cave at dusk to feed. Rarely disturbed by people, some caves have been home to bat colonies for thousands of years.*

◀ *Stalactites hang down like huge icicles from the roofs of caves. They form as water drips down and deposits calcium carbonate. One of the longest stalactites on record measured more than 12 m long. It was in a cave in Brazil.*

▸▸	WORLD'S DEEPEST CAVES		
	CAVE	**COUNTRY**	**DEPTH**
★1	Reseau Jean Bernard	France	1,602 m
2	Lamprechtsofen-Vogelshacht	Austria	1,537 m
3	Gouffre Mirolda/Lucien Bouclier	France	1,520 m

▼ *Stalagmites grow up from the floors of caves as water drips down from the roof and deposits calcium carbonate. A stalagmite more than 30 m tall – higher than a house! – was measured inside a cave in Slovakia.*

VIOLENT VOLCANOES AND GEYSERS

A volcano is a hole in Earth's crust. Hot, melted rocks are pushed out through the hole from time to time. When this happens, the volcano erupts. Active volcanoes erupt often. Dormant volcanoes do so only occasionally. Extinct volcanoes are safely dead and will not erupt again. There are more than 800 known active volcanoes in the world. The country with the most is Indonesia, which has about 200.

▲ *Geysers are spouts of steam and hot water, found in volcanically active regions. In 1903 a New Zealand geyser spurted to 460 m high – the highest ever measured. The tallest geyser 'blowing' today is Steamboat Geyser in Yellowstone National Park, USA, shown here. It blasts out hot steam to a height of about 115 m.*

▼ *A volcano erupts with immense force, sending hot molten rock, ash, steam and gas into the air.*

DID YOU KNOW?
Kilauea, a volcano on Hawaii, is the world's biggest-ever active volcano. Since its most recent outburst began in 1983, it has been spouting fountains of fire and a river of red-hot lava. Hawaii also has the world's biggest volcano. Called Mauna Loa, it rises about 9,000 m from the sea floor. More than 80 percent of Mauna Loa is beneath the ocean.

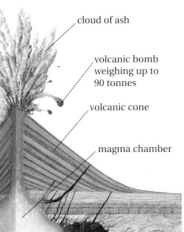

► *Magma, or melted rock, rises up a vent tube from a chamber deep inside the volcano. Lava bursts out like boiling tar and hardens as it cools on the slopes of the volcanic cone. Volcanic bombs of rock are hurled into the air.*

cloud of ash

volcanic bomb weighing up to 90 tonnes

volcanic cone

magma chamber

◄ *The biggest release of noise and energy from a volcano was in 1883, when Krakatoa Island, Indonesia, blew up. The noise was heard up to 5,000 km away, 4 hours later.*

VOLCANO FACTS

Biggest volcano	Mauna Loa	Hawaii	Crater 180 m deep
Highest active volcano	Ojos del Salado	South America	6,887 m high
Most restless volcano	Kilauea	Hawaii	Erupting since 1983

A HUGE DISASTER

● In 1815 the Tambora volcano in Indonesia spewed out nine times more dust, ash and rock than Krakatoa.

● Some 92,000 people were killed by the Tambora volcano, its tidal wave, or by famine afterwards.

► *The most destructive volcano to erupt in North America in recent times was Mount St Helens in Washington state, in 1980. Ash spread over 800 km, avalanches were triggered, and 66 people were killed.*

» Place to avoid: San Andreas fault, California, USA   » Most frightening side-effect: tsunami (tidal wave)

EARTHQUAKES

Earthquakes shake the ground so powerfully that city buildings can topple and bridges and roads can be shattered. The energy released is many times greater than from an atomic bomb. Like volcanoes, earthquakes mostly happen where the plates that make up Earth's crust meet. The movement of the plates puts such stress on the rocks that they break apart. The world's worst earthquake of recent times was in northeast China in 1976, when at least 250,000 people were killed.

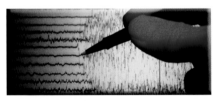

▲ *A seismograph measures the strength and direction of earthquake waves. It records the tremors and compares their strength on the Richter scale. A scale of one is a minor earthquake, while a scale of seven is severe.*

HOW OFTEN DO EARTHQUAKES HAPPEN?

● There are as many as 500,000 earthquakes every year. Luckily most of them are too small to be felt.
● Each year, on average, there are about 1,000 earthquakes that cause damage to buildings.

▼ *Earthquakes (and volcanoes) are most likely to happen along faults in Earth's crust, where two of the plates meet. The movement of the plates puts the rocks from which they are made under such pressure that they can no longer hold together. Massive amounts of energy are released in shock waves as the rocks break apart. The result is an earthquake.*

★	**KILLER EARTHQUAKES**		
	COUNTRY	**DATE**	**KILLED**
1	Egypt	1201	1 million
2	China	1556	830,000
3	India	1737	300,000
4	China	1976	250,000
5	China	1920	200,000
6	Japan	1923	142,000
7	Sicily	1908	75,000
8	Iran	1990	40,000
9	Martinique	1902	38,000
10	Armenia	1988	25,000

▼ *When rock is pushed and pulled in opposite directions by the movement of Earth's crust, it can shear and break apart. A crack along which rocks move is called a fault.*

arrows show movement of land

ocean plate and continental plate meet; the thin crust under the ocean is forced beneath the thicker crust under the mountain range – an earthquake occurs

mountain range

active volcano

movement of land

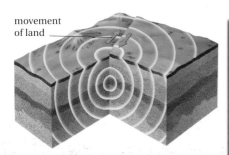

▲ *Shock waves from an earthquake spread out in waves deep below the surface. The point on the surface directly above is called the epicentre. Aftershocks, sometimes hours later, can cause just as much damage.*

1   2

▲ *There are two kinds of surface shock waves: 1) Rayleigh, or R, waves make the ground roll. 2) Love, or Q, waves shake the ground from side to side.*

➤➤ BIG EARTHQUAKES OF THE 20TH CENTURY				
	PLACE	**COUNTRY**	**DATE**	**RICHTER SCALE**
★ 1	Aleutian Islands	USA	1957	9.1
2 =	Assam	India	1950	8.6
2 =	Gansu	China	1920	8.6
3 =	San Francisco	USA	1906	8.3
3 =	Kanto Plain	Japan	1923	8.3
4	Tangshan	China	1976	8.2
5	Mexico City	Mexico	1985	8.1

▶ *It takes a really big earthquake to make cracks open up in the ground. This seismologist is recording the size of the gaps that have appeared.*

◀ *The city of Los Angeles on the west coast of the USA is built on the San Andreas fault, one of the most active faults in the world. The city was badly damaged by an earthquake in 1994.*

▼ *Japan lies on a boundary of two plates. A major earthquake occurs there about every five years. Without special reinforced foundations, few buildings can survive. In 1995 an earthquake in Kobe and Osaka flattened 100,000 buildings – while one in 1923 wrecked five times that number.*

➤➤ EARTHQUAKE STRENGTH ON RICHTER SCALE		
	RICHTER SCALE	**DEGREE OF DAMAGE**
★ 1	11–12	Catastrophic, ground rises and falls in waves
2	8–11	Disastrous, ground cracks, serious damage and loss of life within 200–300 km radius
3	7.0–7.9	Major earthquake, serious damage and loss of life over a large area
4	6.0–6.9	Damage to buildings within 100 km radius
5	5.4–6.0	Major damage to poorly built buildings
6	3.5–5.4	Often felt, but rarely cause damage
7	3–3.5	Tremors felt, like a heavy truck passing

DESERTS

Almost one eighth of Earth's surface is dry desert, receiving less than 250 mm of rainfall in a year. The biggest desert is the Sahara in north Africa, at 5,000 km across and up to 2,250 km north to south. It has the world's biggest sand dunes, some more than 400 m high. Temperatures can be scorching hot by day and near-freezing at night. Not all deserts are sandy though. Most deserts are stony or icy. The continent with the most deserts is Asia.

▲ An oasis is a green 'island' in the desert. Underground water allows plants and trees to grow. Some oases support small towns.

◀ Wind and sand have eroded, or worn away, these famous desert rocks in Monument Valley, Arizona, USA, giving them strange shapes.

▶ The driest place on Earth is the Atacama Desert in Chile, South America. Intervals between showers may be as long as 100 years, and in some areas it has not rained for more than 400 years!

FUR COATS IN THE GOBI

● In the Gobi Desert temperatures drop below freezing for half the year. No wonder the camels in the Gobi have thick woolly coats.

▼ Camels are the most useful desert pack animals. They can live for weeks on a few mouthfuls of thorns or dried leaves, and go for several days without water.

» BIGGEST DESERTS		
DESERT	**LOCATION**	**AREA**
★1 Sahara	North Africa	9 million sq km
2 Australian	Australia	3.8 million sq km
3 Arabian	Southwest Asia	1.3 million sq km
4 Gobi	Central Asia	1 million sq km
5 Kalahari	Southern Africa	520,000 sq km

saguaro cactus

elf owl

elf owl

woodpecker

bat

humming bird

jack rabbit

cactus wren

gila monster

fennec fox

cactus flower

▶ *The vast Sahara takes in 11 countries of northern Africa, including Algeria and Tunisia, where there are 'seas of sand', called ergs.*

▶ *Desert plants such as cacti store water in leaves or stems, and some have very deep roots for finding water underground. They flower and set seeds quickly after rain has fallen. Many desert animals, such as the fennec fox, come out in the cool of night to find food. Some never drink, getting all the moisture they need from their food. Others, like the gila monster, run about in the fierce heat, raising their bodies above the sand to keep as cool as possible.*

SNOW AND ICE

Temperatures at the South Pole fall below those at the North Pole – they can reach -50°C during an Antarctic winter. But the snowiest place in the world is not at either of the poles. It is on the west coast of the United States! During the winter of 1971–72, Paradise, in the mountains of Washington state, received 31,000 mm of snow. The deepest snowfall ever measured was in nearby California, also on the west coast of the USA, where in 1911 snow lay 11.46 m deep – enough to bury a house.

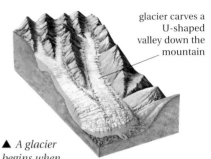

glacier carves a U-shaped valley down the mountain

▲ *A glacier begins when winter snow fills a high mountain basin, forming a mass of ice. The basin overflows and the ice slides down the mountain in a slow 'river of ice'.*

◀ *The biggest hailstone fell in Coffeyville, Kansas, USA, in 1970. It was 44.5 cm round, and weighed nearly 1 kg – bigger and much heavier than a tennis ball. Freak hailstones have been known to kill.*

▼ *The frozen waters of Antarctica support huge colonies, or rookeries, of fish-eating penguins and several kinds of seal.*

▲ *The ice covering Greenland is about 1.5 km thick, but the ice in Antarctica, shown here, is three times thicker, at up to 4.8 km thick! Scientists measure it by using echo-sounding equipment.*

southern elephant seals (bull, cow and pup)

LONGEST GLACIERS

	GLACIER	LOCATION		LENGTH
1	Lambert-Fisher	Antarctica		515 km
2	Novaya Zemlya	Russia		418 km
3	Arctic Institute	Antarctica		362 km

Note: Eight of the ten longest glaciers in the world are in Antarctica

◀ *An iceberg is a huge chunk of ice in the sea that has broken off a glacier. Big icebergs tower 120 m above the sea – but this may be only one-ninth of the total ice. The rest is under the water.*

▲ *The most snow to fall in 24 hours was 1.93 m in Silver Lake, Colorado, USA, in 1921. It was enough to cover a tall, upright man from head to foot.*

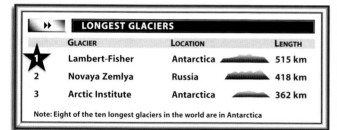

▲ *Roald Amundsen of Norway led the first expedition to the South Pole in 1911.*

ANTARCTIC ICEBERGS

● Antarctic icebergs are flatter than Arctic ones.
● The biggest iceberg was spotted in the Antarctic in 1956. It was 335 km long and 97 km across. Belgium would have fitted on top of it!

▲ *Permafrost is frozen soil that never thaws. The thickest permafrost was measured in Siberia in 1982, and was 1,370 m deep. Deep-frozen, extinct mammoths are dug out of the Siberian permafrost from time to time!*

adult emperor penguin

Adélie penguin

young penguin

Weddell seal and pup

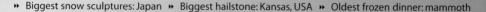

WEATHER

Regular weather charts have been kept for only about the last 250 years, and accurate temperature readings date from the 1800s. But people have always liked talking about weather. Chinese histories show that 903 BC was a very bad winter in China, and the Romans commented on the weather when they landed in Britain in 55 BC. The 7th century in England was unusually warm, while the winter of 1683–84 was so cold that the River Thames froze. The 1990s had several of the hottest years recorded in the 20th century.

▲ *Most rainbows last for only a few minutes, but the longest lasted for up to 6 hours. A rainbow forms when sunlight is bent and split by raindrops into the colours of the spectrum that make up light: violet, indigo, blue, green, yellow, orange and red.*

» WEATHER RECORDS			
Hottest place	Death Valley, California, USA	Above 49°C for 43 days	1917
Hottest all-year-round	Dallol, Ethiopia	34°C average	1960–66
Highest temperature	Al Aziziyah, Libya	58°C	1922
Highest-measured wind speed	New Hampshire, USA	371 km/h	1934
Coldest place	Vostok base, Antarctica	-89.2°C	1983

◄ *In the tropics, the region spanning the Equator, the weather is hot and wet all year round, and there are no seasons. Rainfall in the tropics can be incredibly heavy, falling at about 32 km/h! Many fruits, such as bananas, coconuts, mangoes and pineapples, flourish in the warm, wet tropical conditions.*

▲ *Much of North America, Europe and far eastern Asia has mild weather and spring and autumn seasons. In autumn the leaves of the 'deciduous' trees turn to brilliant colours, and in winter they drop off.*

» Longest-lasting rainbow: 6 hours » Sunniest city: Yuma, Arizona, USA » Driest region: coast of Chile

▶ The aurora borealis, or Northern Lights, makes the night sky glow green, gold, red or purple. The effect is caused by solar wind – radiation from the Sun – hitting Earth's atmosphere.

▲ All of Earth's weather, including clouds, is produced in the lowest layer of the atmosphere, called the troposphere. The troposphere extends to about 15 km above the surface of Earth. In the next layer up, the stratosphere, a thin layer of 'ozone' blocks the harmful radiation from the Sun.

MAP KEY
- Polar
- Cool temperate
- Mountains
- Warm temperate
- Tropical
- Desert and semidesert

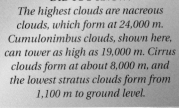

DID YOU KNOW?
The highest clouds are nacreous clouds, which form at 24,000 m. Cumulonimbus clouds, shown here, can tower as high as 19,000 m. Cirrus clouds form at about 8,000 m, and the lowest stratus clouds form from 1,100 m to ground level.

▶ On Mount Wai-'ale-'ale in Hawaii you need an umbrella on all but 15 days of the year, while a record 38 mm of rain fell in one minute in Guadeloupe in the West Indies in 1970!

▼ The USA (not counting Alaska) has about 105 major snowstorms a year, and its snowiest major city is Buffalo, New York state. It is thought that no two snowflakes are the same!

STORM FORCES

Storms are extremes of weather, ranging from hailstorms and blizzards to sandstorms and duststorms. The most destructive storms are hurricanes, known as cyclones in the Indian Ocean and typhoons in the Pacific Ocean. Wind strength is measured by the Beaufort scale. A scale of one is light air movement, while a scale of 12 is hurricane force. Hurricane winds can spiral at more than 400 km/h around a calm centre, called the 'eye'. Hurricanes cause terrible damage on land, as do tornadoes, or twisters, which are common in the United States. At sea, tornadoes create whirling waterspouts.

»	BEAUFORT SCALE	
	WIND FORCE	**WIND SPEED**
1 ★	12 Hurricane	118+ km/h
2	11 Violent storm	103–117 km/h
3	10 Storm	89–102 km/h
4	9 Strong gale	75–88 km/h
5	8 Gale	62–74 km/h
6	7 Near gale	50–61 km/h
7	6 Strong breeze	39–49 km/h
8	5 Fresh breeze	29–38 km/h
9	4 Moderate breeze	20–28 km/h
10	3 Gentle breeze	12–19 km/h
11	2 Light breeze	6–11 km/h
12	1 Light air	1–5 km/h
13	0 Calm	1 km/h

◀ Britain's worst storm of modern times was the hurricane of October, 1987. High winds uprooted and blew down 15 million trees in southern England, blocked roads, and brought down roofs and power lines.

◀ The winds are influenced by the spinning of Earth. Either side of the Equator there are steady winds, called 'trade winds' by sailors. Between the trade winds lie the gentler doldrums. Westerly winds are common the farther north or south of the Equator you go, while in the polar regions easterly winds prevail.

»	WEATHER RECORDS
Most thunder	Tororo, Uganda, Africa – average of 250 thundery days a year
Worst hailstorm	A hailstorm in 1888 battered to death 246 people in India
Highest waterspout	A waterspout 1,500 m high was seen off New South Wales, Australia, in 1888
Hottest flash	Lightning heats the air around it to more than 33,000°C – five times hotter than the Sun
Worst cyclone	In 1991, 138,000 people were killed when a cyclone and tidal wave hit Bangladesh
Worst hurricane	Hurricane Flora in 1963 killed 6,000 people in the Caribbean

▶ Thunderclouds build up to great heights, dark and laden with rain. Thunder is the sound air makes when it expands, warmed by the heat of a lightning flash. Because sound travels more slowly than light, we see the lightning seconds before we hear the clap of thunder.

▼ *A tornado can lift and scatter cars as if they were toys, and can literally burst a building apart from the inside.*

◀ *A tornado is a windstorm that creates a huge funnel of whirling air stretching down to the ground. The tip of the funnel sucks up everything in its track. In the United States tornadoes are called 'twisters'. They roar across the Midwest at speeds of 50 km/h.*

◀ *Hurricanes form over the Atlantic Ocean and move westward through the Caribbean and across the southern United States. Most years, such giant storms strike the coasts, flattening trees and buildings, flooding towns and wrecking communications.*

◀ *When a hurricane hits, many people lose the roofs of their homes. Floods can do as much damage as the high winds.*

◀ *Satellites in space track hurricanes over the ocean, and so provide early warning for people to move to safety. You can even watch a hurricane's progress live on the Internet.*

RAINING FISH

● Storm winds create strong up-draughts of air over water that can suck up fish and frogs. The animals rain down from the sky, to the surprise of people below!

PLANET EARTH *QUIZ*

Now that you have read all about what's biggest and best on Planet Earth, see if you can answer these 20 quiz questions! (Pictures give clues, answers at the top of the page.)

▶ *4. Which canal links the Mediterranean and Red Seas?*

▼ *2. Which is the biggest ocean?*

▼ *5. Which country has the longest coastline?*

▲ *1. What is Earth's centre called?*

▲ *3. What substance covers 71 percent of Earth's surface?*

▼ *7. Where is the highest waterfall in the world?*

▲ *6. Which famous waterfall lies on the border between the USA and Canada?*

◀ *9. Which is the longest mountain range in the world?*

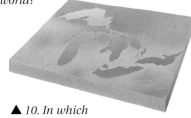

▲ *8. Which is the longest river?*

▲ *10. In which continent are the Great Lakes?*

» 1.The inner core » 2.The Pacific » 3.Water » 4.The Suez Canal » 5.Canada » 6.Niagara Falls
» 11.Lake Baikal » 12.Greenland » 13.France » 14.Edmund Hillary and Tenzing Norgay » 15.San Andreas Fault

▼ 11. Which lake is deeper than any other and is home to these seals?

▲ 12. Which is the biggest island?

▲ 13. The Lascaux cave paintings are found in which country?

▼ 14. Name the first two men to climb Mount Everest.

▲ 17. Which country has the most active volcanoes?

▲ 16. Do stalactites grow up or hang down in caves?

▼ 18. Name the first explorer to reach the South Pole.

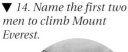

▲ 15. Los Angeles lies on which famous fault?

▼ 19. What is the driest place on Earth?

► 20. Where can the thickest ice be found?

INDEX

**Entries in bold refer to
illustrations**

*The publishers wish to thank the following artists
who have contributed to this book:*
Andy Beckett, Kuo Kang Chen, Jeremy Gower, Gary Hincks,
Richard Hook, Rob Jakeway, Janos Marffy, Guy Smith, Roger Smith,
Rudi Vizi, Mike White, John Woodcock

*The publishers wish to thank the following sources
for the photographs used in this book:*
CORBIS: Page 17 (B/R) Marc Garanger; Page 17 (R) Shai Ginott;
Page 19 (B/R) Ralph A. Clevenger; Page 20 (B/L) Craig Lovell;
Page 22 (R) David Muench; Page 26 (T/R) Charles O'Rear
All other photographs from Miles Kelly Archives